W9-DGB-524

Influenza

by Beth Bence Reinke

PEBBLE
a capstone imprint

Pebble Explore is published by Pebble, an imprint of Capstone.
1710 Roe Crest Drive
North Mankato, Minnesota 56003
www.capstonepub.com

Library of Congress Cataloging-in-Publication Data
Names: Bence Reinke, Beth, author.
Title: Influenza / by Beth Bence Reinke.
Description: North Mankato, Minnesota : Pebble, [2022] | Series: Health and my body | Includes bibliographical references and index. | Audience: Ages 5-8 | Audience: Grades K-1 | Summary: "Each year, the influenza virus causes illness in people around the world. The virus can spread quickly, but there are ways to help keep it at bay. Expertly leveled text and vibrant photos will help kids learn to recognize and prevent Influenza"— Provided by publisher.
Identifiers: LCCN 2021002528 (print) | LCCN 2021002529 (ebook) | ISBN 9781663908155 (hardcover) | ISBN 9781663921024 (paperback) | ISBN 9781663908124 (pdf) | ISBN 9781663908148 (kindle edition)
Subjects: LCSH: Influenza—Juvenile literature. | Influenza—Prevention—Juvenile literature. | Influenza—Treatment—Juvenile literature.
Classification: LCC RA644.I6 B46 2022 (print) | LCC RA644.I6 (ebook) | DDC 614.5/18—dc23
LC record available at https://lccn.loc.gov/2021002528
LC ebook record available at https://lccn.loc.gov/2021002529

Image Credits
Alamy: ZUMA Press Inc, 17; iStockphoto: PaulGregg, 9; Science Source: Hazel Appleton, Health Protection Agency Centre for Infections, 7; Shutterstock: cabania, 21, Daisy Daisy, 25, DG PhotoStock, 23, Inside Creative House, 29, Irina Borsuchenko, 19, Krakenimages.com, 27, Motortion Films, 11, New Africa, 15, pavla, 5, photonova, design element, Primeiya, Cover, Prostock-studio, 13

Editorial Credits
Editor: Gena Chester; Designer: Kazuko Collins; Media Researcher: Jo Miller; Production Specialist: Tori Abraham

Printed and bound in China.   4205

Table of Contents

Words in **bold** are in the glossary.

What Is Influenza?

Influenza is an infection of the body's **airways**. It's caused by a tiny germ called a **virus**. The influenza virus attacks the nose and throat. It often infects the lungs too.

Influenza is also called "the flu." There are three main types of flu viruses. They are types A, B, and C.

The flu virus attacks
the body's airways.

Types A and B can cause severe illness. There are many kinds of type A flu viruses. Type A can infect humans and some animals. Horses, pigs, and birds can get type A flu. Types B and C flu viruses only infect people. Type C only causes mild **symptoms**.

New flu viruses often develop. Sometimes they cause **pandemics**. A pandemic is a period of time when an illness spreads to people all around the world. In 1918, there was a flu pandemic. The most recent flu pandemic was in 2009.

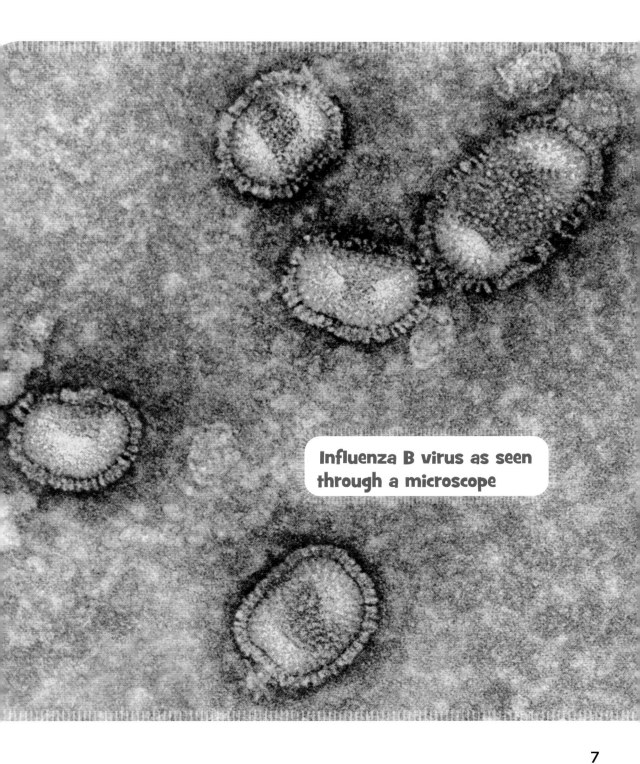

Influenza B virus as seen through a microscope

How the Flu Spreads

The flu is **contagious**. It spreads from person to person. Millions of Americans get sick during flu season. It lasts from late fall to spring. But most people get the flu in winter.

Influenza viruses spread in tiny droplets. The droplets spread in two ways. They move through the air. They also land on objects.

Say you sneeze into the air. Achoo! Droplets spray from your nose. They fly out of your mouth when you cough too.

The droplets can land on other people. The virus gets in their noses, eyes, or mouths. Then they might get sick with the flu.

Droplets can land on things. Flu viruses can stay on these things for about two days. Other people touch the objects. They get the virus on their hands. Then they rub their eyes. Or they touch their nose or mouth.

Then the flu virus gets into their body. It takes over cells in the airways. The cells make many more viruses. About two days later, the person has symptoms of the flu.

Your Body and the Flu

Anyone can get the flu. Babies can get very sick. Pregnant women can too. Adults over 65 can have severe flu symptoms. So can people with heart or lung problems.

Flu symptoms come on fast. You usually get a high fever with the flu. You may shiver from chills. Your whole body aches, even your head. You get a cough and sore throat. Your nose may be stuffy. And you feel very tired.

There are many symptoms of the flu.

Kids can have extra flu symptoms. They might throw up. They may have diarrhea. But adults don't often get those symptoms.

The flu lasts about a week. But some symptoms can stay with you. Your cough may last longer. You may feel tired for almost a month.

The flu can also cause other infections. Some people get ear infections. Others get a serious infection in their lungs called pneumonia.

Treating the Flu

Doctors can usually tell if you have the flu. They know because of your symptoms. But sometimes they do a flu test to be sure.

A nurse swabs your nose. The swab gathers **mucus**. Scientists test the mucus. The test shows if you have the flu. Results may be ready in a few hours.

A medical professional can give someone a flu test.

If you have the flu, take care of yourself. Get plenty of sleep. Resting helps your body fight the virus.

Fluids help keep your body strong. Drink a lot of water. You can drink hot tea or broth. Hot drinks help loosen mucus. They unclog your nose. Cold drinks soothe your throat. Try a smoothie or freeze pop.

Humid air helps you breathe easier. Use a warm mist **humidifier**. Or breathe steam from a hot shower.

Drinking hot tea helps ease flu symptoms.

Medicine

Medicine doesn't make the flu go away. But it helps you feel better. Some medicines lower your fever. They can ease your body aches too. Other kinds help your cough. A trusted adult can give you medicine.

A doctor may give you **antiviral** medicine. It works best in the first two days of the flu. This medicine does not cure the flu. But it helps you get better faster.

Medicine can help people feel better,
but it cannot cure the flu.

Preventing the Flu

The flu spreads easily. But you can help stop the spread. If you are sick, stay home.

Don't share food or drinks. Cover your sneezes and coughs. Cough into your elbow. Keep tissues nearby. Sneeze into them. Wash your hands after.

Hot water destroys the flu virus. So do cleaning products. A trusted adult can help you clean things. They can wipe down things you touched. They can wash your towels and sheets.

Wash your hands often. Washing gets rid of the flu virus. Use warm water and soap. Rub your palms together. Wash the tops of your hands. Scrub between your fingers. Get your fingernails clean too.

It takes 20 seconds to get your hands clean. Singing a song helps you wash long enough. Sing the "Happy Birthday" song twice. Hum the "ABCs" song. Try counting to 20 slowly.

Staying Well

Staying healthy can help fight the flu virus. You can help your body stay well. Follow these tips:

Get plenty of sleep. Kids need 10 hours each night. Your body heals during sleep.

Eat healthy foods. Fruits and vegetables help keep you well. Eat some of each every day.

Get exercise each day. Moving your body makes it strong.

Try not to worry. Stress is bad for your health.

Eating vegetables helps keep you healthy.

Vaccines

The flu **vaccine** helps prevent influenza. It's a liquid that contains parts of flu viruses. The flu vaccine is safe for most people over 6 months old.

Scientists create a new flu vaccine every year. That's because flu viruses change. It's important to get a flu vaccine every year.

The vaccine is given in a shot. It goes in your arm. The vaccine can also be in a spray. It goes in your nose. Your doctor knows which type is best for you.

It takes two weeks for the vaccine to work. It helps your body make **antibodies**. Antibodies fight the flu virus. They are an important step in staying healthy.

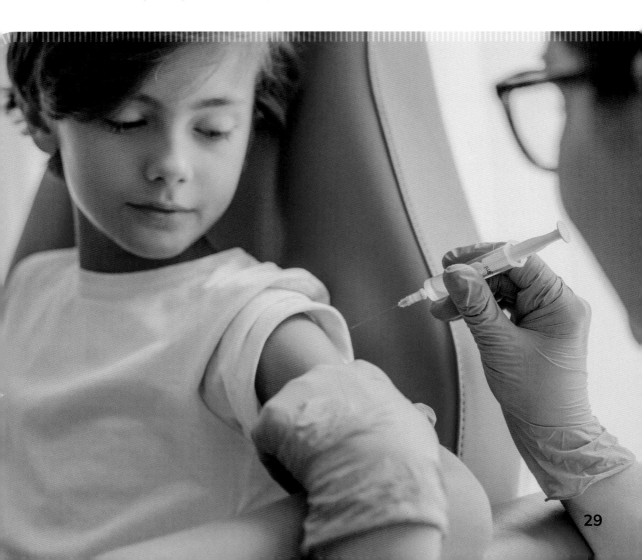

Glossary

airway (ERH-way)—a breathing passage such as the nose, throat, and lungs

antibody (AN-tih-bah-dee)—a substance in the body that fights against infection and disease

antiviral (an-ty-VY-rul)—describes a drug that fights a virus

contagious (kun-TAY-juss)—easy to spread

humidifier (hyoo-mid-uh-FYE-ur)—a device used to create and keep damp air in a room

mucus (MYOO-kuhss)—liquid made by cells inside the nose and breathing passages

pandemic (pan-DEM-ik)—a disease outbreak that spreads across the world

symptom (SIMP-tum)—a sign the body shows when it is sick

virus (VY-rus)—a tiny germ that can make people sick

vaccine (vak-SEEN)—a substance that helps the body protect itself from a specific germ

Read More

Borgert-Spaniol, Megan. *All About the Flu.* Minneapolis: ABDO, 2019.

Hopkinson, Deborah. *The Deadliest Diseases Then and Now.* New York: Scholastic Press, 2021.

Krasner, Barbara. *Influenza: How the Flu Changed History.* North Mankato, MN: Capstone, 2019.

Internet Sites

KidsHealth: Flu
kidshealth.org/en/kids/flu.html

KidsHealth: The Flu: Should You Go to School?
kidshealth.org/en/kids/h1n1-school.html

KidsHealth: The Flu: Stop the Spread
kidshealth.org/en/kids/flu-spread.html

Index

WITHDRAWN